DATE DUE

OCT 15 2003			
GAYLORD			PRINTED IN U.S.A.

I want to be a Police Officer

I WANT TO BE A
Police Officer

DAN LIEBMAN

FIREFLY BOOKS

A FIREFLY BOOK

Published by Firefly Books Ltd. 2000

First Printing

Cataloguing in Publication Data

Liebman, Daniel
    I want to be a police officer

ISBN 1-55209-467-7 (bound)   ISBN 1-55209-465-0 (pbk.)

1. Police – Juvenile literature.   I. Title

HV7922.L53 2000   j363.2'2   C99-932463-2

Published in Canada in 2000 by
Firefly Books Ltd.
3680 Victoria Park Avenue
Willowdale, Ontario, Canada
M2H 3K1

Published in the United States in 2000 by
Firefly Books (U.S.) Inc.
P.O. Box 1338, Ellicott Station
Buffalo, New York, USA
14205

Photo Credits

© Benn Mitchell, The Image Bank, front cover.
© Jeff Hunter, The Image Bank, page 5.
© Robert Maass/CORBIS, pages 6-7.
© Neil Beer/CORBIS, page 8.
© Yellow Dog Productions, The Image Bank, page 9.
© Grant V. Faint, The Image Bank, page 10.
© Karl Weatherly/CORBIS, page 11.
© Al Harvey, page 12.
© Gary Gladstone Studio, The Image Bank, page 13.
© Andy Caulfield, The Image Bank, pages 14-15.
© David W. Hamilton, The Image Bank, page 16.
© James Marshall/CORBIS, page 17.
© David H. Wells/CORBIS, pages 18-19.
© Tom Nebbia/CORBIS, page 20.
© Tom Nebbia/CORBIS, page 21.
© Barros & Barros, The Image Bank, page 22.
© G.S. & V. Chapman, The Image Bank, page 23.
© CORBIS, page 24.

Design by Interrobang Graphic Design Inc.
Printed and bound in Canada by Friesens, Altona, Manitoba

Canada
The Publisher acknowledges the financial support of the Government of Canada through the Book Publishing Industry Development Program for its publishing activities.

Police officers enjoy helping people. They make sure that the laws are obeyed.

THOMAS

Police are able to do their jobs better when they make friends with the people in the neighbourhood.

Because many police officers work outdoors, they must wear heavy jackets on cold winter days.

Officers carry their equipment with them – sometimes right on their belts. They can always call for help.

Motorcycles go many places where a car cannot travel. They let officers move quickly through busy streets.

Bicycles come in handy, too. They are especially useful in crowded cities during the summer.

Some lucky police even get to ride horses. These officers are patrolling a city park.

Police inspect cars and trucks to make sure they are safe to drive.

Help is on the way! Sirens and flashing lights warn everyone that this police car is in a big hurry.

Rangers are officers who patrol forests and large parks.

Cities on oceans, rivers and large lakes often need harbor police to patrol the water.

From high above, an officer can look down on a large area of the city.

Police dogs can do things that humans can't. Their sensitive noses can find explosives, lost children or a criminal who is hiding.

The dogs and their partners work hard. But great friends make a great team.

An important part of the job is keeping records of accidents and crimes.

Police scientists examine clues to solve crimes. This fingerprint might tell them who robbed a bank.

To be an officer you need a lot of skills. You have to think fast, use proper judgment and know how to use the latest equipment.